# HOW I SAVED

# MY MARRIAGE

## Anger management   practice for wives.

**Carla.G.Taylor**

# Table of contents

Chapter 1: EFFECTIVE COMMUNICATION IN A MARRIAGE

Chapter two: How to Be a Better Wife and Improve Your Marriage?

Chapter Three: Parenting

Chapter 4:How to make your weekends better with your kids.

Chapter five: 10 Ways to Strengthen a Marriage and Avoid Divorce

# Chapter 1: EFFECTIVE COMMUNICATION IN A MARRIAGE

The significance of correspondence in marriage is much of the time not viewed in a serious way as many couples will generally believe that the everyday exchange or its absence doesn't influence them on an everyday premise. Be that as it may, correspondence is the vehicle through which any remaining significant pieces of marriage are performed.

In the event that you love somebody, yet you don't utilise your words and your activities to convey it, you're not doing a good job for your accomplice. In the event that you trust somebody, let them in on it. Marriage and correspondence ought to remain closely connected.

In the event that you can impart it, your marriage has a decent possibility of being cheerful and sound. As a matter of fact, the significance of correspondence ought to be viewed as right from the romance days as it sets the right underpinning of the relationship.

Research lets us know that open a couple correspondence is the foundation of every long and cherishing marriage. The issue is that certain individuals simply aren't great at it.

Love, trust, genuineness, and each and every significant trait of a solid marriage aren't significant in themselves. The outflow of these things creates a marriage worth begrudging.

Showing that affection, exhibiting your trust, and acting sincerely is where the enchantment is. Having the option to convey how much your better half or spouse means to you is where your marriage goes from great to extraordinary.

However, correspondence in marriage is something other than talking. Let the standards of marriage correspondence guide the closeness, love and sound association in your marriage.

## Kinds of correspondence in marriage

While correspondence is significant, it doesn't necessarily allude to the demonstration of verbally conversing with your accomplice about your sentiments, your day, your past or expectations and fears about what's to come.

Correspondence can happen without a solitary word being verbally expressed. Here are the various types of correspondence in marriage that can improve your marriage:

• **Verbal correspondence**

Everybody likes to hear that they look decent. Everybody likes to hear that they are cherished. Verbal correspondence is having the option to communicate how you feel to your companion through the words that you express, making it fundamental for successful couple correspondence.

In the event that you love somebody with your entire being, yet you don't say it enough, the other individual might very well never see exactly how profoundly they are cherished. Having the option to let your life partner know how brilliant they are will cause them to feel cherished, appreciated, and in contact with how you feel.

So in the event that you comprehend the significance of correspondence in marriage, you won't take verbal marriage relational abilities with your accomplice gently. Such kind of openness is of the utmost importance for a drawn out relationship.

Alongside articulations of joy, you must have the option to shout out about what you're not content with. Assuming your life partner is doing something that irritates you profoundly, yet you're quiet regarding the matter, your absence of correspondence and belief will just permit the activity to proceed.

couple taking and having espresso together

You can't carry on with existence with your significant other or spouse holding all of your disappointment inside. Letting it out is vital and good for your relationship. This ought to be finished in a thoughtful and warm way, however don't hold on until offering something that you really want to is past the point of no return.

• **Non-verbal correspondence**

At the point when we discuss the significance of correspondence in marriage, we can't underplay nonverbal correspondence. Us people say much more with our bodies than we give ourselves credit for.

Know about how your non-verbal communication is speaking Jm your accomplice. Face your better half or spouse and keep your non-verbal communication open while having troublesome discussions.

Assuming you're slouched over and shut off while attempting to have a significant discussion, your accomplice will subliminally feel that absence of weakness.

No leg crossing. No arm crossing. Your body ought to show your companion that you are available to hear what they need to say and will manage it.

There are a lot of nonverbal signals like a shut off act that are conveying either adversely or decidedly to your accomplice with no words being traded. Be more cognizant and smart about how your body communicates your sentiments.

• **Actual demonstrations**

Making supper. Going to the supermarket. Taking out the trash. Going on a frozen yoghourt run for your pregnant spouse. These aren't things that you say; they are things that you do that show your companion that you care about them.

In doing little and smart demonstrations, you are imparting your adoration for your companion without expressing much by any stretch of the imagination. At the point when we discuss the significance of correspondence in connections, such actual demonstrations go quite far for couples who may not be that extraordinary with verbal correspondence.

The expression "talk is cheap" fits suitably with this type of correspondence. Show your companion, through your non-verbal communication, that you are telling the truth and open with them.

Be aware of what your body is talking about, and make the legitimate changes so your significant other or spouse realises that you're being veritable. Cutting off yourself, covering your mouth when you talk, and making negative looks are warnings to the attentive eye.

couple clasping hands

Utilise your activities to convey your adoration, trust, and genuineness with your accomplice. Get them an insightful gift, give them a back rub, or help them with a disturbing errand. Words don't need to be spoken; your activities will represent themselves.

Correspondence is the bedrock of a sound marriage. In any case, the nature of discussions matter in a marriage, as opposed to how much time that you spend conversing with one another.

## 1.Be explicit.

At the point when issues emerge, be explicit. Wide speculations as, "You do it constantly!" are not useful.

Stay away from mind-perusing.
It is extremely disappointing when another person behaves like they understand better compared to you what you were truly thinking.

## 2.**Express gloomy sentiments productively**.

There will be times when you feel sharpness, disdain, dissatisfaction or objection. These sentiments should be conveyed for change to happen. In any case, how you offer these viewpoints is basic. It's one comment, "I'm truly frustrated that you are burning the midnight oil again this evening." But assuming you say, "You plainly couldn't care less about me or the children. Assuming you did, you wouldn't work late consistently," will convey something else.

Tune in without being guarded.
For a union to succeed, the two companions should have the option to hear each other's grumblings without getting cautious. This is a lot harder than figuring out how to really communicate pessimistic sentiments.

## 3.**Uninhibitedly express good sentiments.**

A great many people are speedier to communicate gloomy sentiments than positive ones. It is imperative to the wellbeing of your marriage that you confirm your companion. Good sentiments like appreciation, fondness, regard, reverence, and endorsement resemble putting aside instalments into your adoration account. You ought to have five positive stores for each one negative. Assuming your commendations surpass your grumblings, your companion will focus on your complaints. Assuming your grievances surpass your commendations, your analysis will fail to attract anyone's attention.

## 4.Keep away from and battle misconceptions

Correspondence among a couple can help as a shield against conjugal errors. At the point when you share their viewpoints, pasts, wants and feelings with one another transparently, your mate can comprehend you better.

Correspondence in marriage can assist you with forestalling a misconception by offering you the chance to figure out your life partner's perspectives and reasons completely. It guarantees that their activities, words and considerations then don't come as a shock to you.

Furthermore, conjugal correspondence is the best technique to unravel yourself from any misconception that might have been created between you and your mate. By making sense of and opening dependent upon one another, you can prevent any misconception from harming your relationship.

## 5. Collects regard

An individual who will be open and open to their sentiments, contemplations and past is somebody you can regard. Your accomplice's personal weakness will give you an effect on their perspective and what propels them. It might convince you to regard their activities, words, encounters and qualities.

Assuming you decide to share the hardships that you have survived, your accomplice will actually want to regard your solidarity and perseverance.

Trust is critical in any relationship as it guarantees unwavering quality, receptiveness and genuine association between two individuals.

Research shows that trust is critical when seeing someone; it guarantees powerful commitment among you and your life partner. Also, in the event that your accomplice is defenceless and open while speaking with you, you will actually want to effectively trust them more.

Consistent correspondence can assist with upgrading a marriage over the long haul, so get to know one another by imparting great verbally, non-verbally or through signals.

You can chip away at further developing Communication in marriage as it will assist you with trying not to burn through your time, exertion and genuine serenity in attempting to think about what your accomplice needs. Also, you can do likewise for your life partner.

Without a trace of successful conjugal correspondence, you and your accomplice will invest your energy attempting to think about what your accomplice likes, how they feel or what might goad them. Mystery would likewise bring about significant blunders that can hurt your relationship.

Straightforwardly asking your accomplice for their perspective can assist you with making the best choice and furthermore let your accomplice in on that you esteem their viewpoint.

## 6. Efficient device

Conveying in a marriage is a compelling approach to finishing things and planning with one another. The work that it expects to be open might appear to be depleting, nonetheless, it is preferred and less tedious over correcting botches when you attempt to do things along with your mate.

Rather than with nothing to do battling about inconsequential things, you can rather converse with your accomplice about things that irritate you and the purpose for this. It will require less investment and will likewise be less distressing to manage.

## 7. Figure out yourself

Correspondence and marriage together may seem like components that meet up to improve the relationship you have with your accomplice. Notwithstanding, there is one more aspect to this affiliation.

Correspondence in marriage can assist you with becoming a superior figuring out how you feel and what makes a difference to you.

Preceding being examined regarding specific things, you might not have gotten an opportunity to think how you feel about them. Hence, conveying can assist you with grasping your own self better.

## 8. Improve conjugal fulfilment

Assuming you are pondering, "For what reason is correspondence significant in a marriage," view at the examinations that consider it to be a significant figure deciding conjugal fulfilment.

Correspondence can assist you with feeling associated with your accomplice and guarantee that you feel fulfilled in your relationship. Your accomplice will be your partner assuming you talk transparently and that guarantees proceeded with interest in the other.

## 9. Become together

Couples can either become separated with time or become together.

To guarantee that couples develop together they ought to keep the lines of correspondence open consistently. In the event that you begin feeling and acting in an unexpected way, discussion with you will keep your accomplice informed about these changes.

couple snickering together

You may chip away at further building communication in marriage as it will assist you with trying not to burn through your time, energy and real peacefulness in attempting to think about what your partner requires. Furthermore, you can do the equivalent for your life mate.

Without even a sign of plausible conjugal correspondence, you and your accomplice will waste your energy attempting to think about what your accomplice loves, how they feel or what can irritate them. Mystery would likewise bring about important blunders that might ruin your partnership.

Straightforwardly requesting your accomplice for their perspective will assist you with making the greatest selection and also let your accomplice in on that you appreciate their viewpoint.

## 10. Learn new things

Do you have a comprehensive insight of your accomplice's past? Might you like to realise them astonishingly better? On the off chance that indeed, continue to disclose.

Discussions with your accomplice will allow you the opportunity to continue to find new things about your life partner. Regardless of the fact that you are so near your accomplice, there will be in every case little subtleties that you will find about your accomplice and comprehend them better.

Correspondence is vital for any effective marriage, however you can't depend on only one of the three different ways recorded previously. It will take a decent equilibrium of verbal, non-verbal and actual correspondence to show your mate the amount they mean to you over the long haul.

Let your life partner know what you love about them, yet additionally don't hesitate for even a moment to voice your viewpoint on the off chance that something is irritating you. That transparent verbal correspondence will turn into a speculation with a tremendous return as the years go by.

Customs to Improve Your Communication in Marriage

In the event that anyone queries you what the real cornerstone from a joyful married existence is, you can respond with love, duty, trustworthiness and other things like this. In any event, how frequently do we mention the value of correspondence in a marriage? Since two persons are investing the great majority of their efforts beneath one rooftop, doesn't indicate that they discuss well with one another. To encourage a pleasant marriage and have areas of strength for a with your life spouse, it is important that there is successful correspondence between the two. Correspondence isn't simply about words; regarding acts or non-verbal correspondence bears tremendous value as well.

**Significance of communication in a marriage.**

Why is correspondence so vital to have a long, satisfying relationship with your significant other? What is the job of correspondence in marriage? All things considered, here are a few focuses that underline the significance of correspondence in marriage:

**1. No Communication Implies No Interest**

 In the event that you don't have the foggiest idea what's going on in your accomplice's life or what issues they might be managing, you will most likely be unable to comprehend or identify. This would gradually prompt an indifference for one another's lives and consequently, stressed connections; hence, having viable communication is significant.

**2. Better Understanding**

Couples who frequently talk, examine their lives or speak with each routinely not just have a superior comprehension with one another, yet it likewise assists them with having a more grounded bond with one another. At the point when you comprehend your life partner and the circumstances they might manage, there would be lesser extension for misconception or equivocalness. **3. Better Marital Satisfaction**

On the off chance that you have opened the entryways of viable correspondence with your life partner, you are bound to encounter a cheerful and serene relationship. Better correspondence implies better fulfilment in a relationship in which you examine everything with one another and hence lesser battles or fights.

## 4. Better Trust, Honesty and Respect

Marriage is a two-way road, you can't simply continue anticipating all that without giving. Subsequently, in the event that you are straightforward with your life partner and give and get positive criticism or offer different issues with complete genuineness, it assists in working with better confidence in a relationship.

## 5. Better Connection

Correspondence is an approach to communicating your sentiments and feelings towards your mate. We comprehend that it doesn't mean much to communicate in words the adoration and love that you have for your mate. Notwithstanding, being expressive and vocal is one of the most mind-blowing approaches to showing your feelings towards your companion, which would prompt a superior association. better association.

**Mistakes Couples Make in a Marriage and How to Solve Them.**

Here are a few normal missteps that the vast majority of us generally make and how we can tackle them really:

**1. More 'Me' in a Marriage**

At the point when you get hitched, the relationship is for both of you. Nonetheless, now and again we might fail to remember that, and marriage turns out to be more about you than about your life partner. For instance, on your commemoration consistently, you believe that your better half should cause you to feel unique and take you out to supper, you would possibly design an occasion when you can disappear, you would go just to places you like, and so on. This shows that your joy or assent is a higher priority than your accomplice. Instructions to Resolve You should consider your accomplice's advantages as well. This would be conceivable when you discuss better with one another.

Converse with your accomplice and understand what they like or abhorrence, or what their concept of festivity or other such things is.

## 2. Yelling at The Spouse

Each relationship has its promising and less promising times, and these will undoubtedly occur. Be that as it may, on the off chance that your companion commits an error regardless of how insignificant or grave it will be, it isn't appropriate to yell or direct frightful sentiments toward your life partner. It is basic to comprehend that no one's perfect, and when you yell or reprimand your mate, you express frightful things. Words expressed out of resentment frequently scar the other individual's sentiments or feelings and it tends to be more obvious when there is less or no correspondence in a marriage. Step by step instructions to Resolve Regardless of whether you have an admirable statement to fly off the handle, don't be. Ensure you inconspicuously put across your point without making any evil sentiments or cynicism. Best is, you hold on until you let your outrage die and afterward converse with your companion about it. The point isn't to show dismay or disillusionment, yet it is about not committing a similar error once more.

### 3.Do Not Compare or Compete

Perhaps the silliest misstep that wedded couples can make is contrasting or contending with their mate. This misstep might be more articulated or clear in individuals with comparative expert foundations or occupations. You might boast about your expert accomplishments or achievements with your companion or discuss their disappointments or misfortunes adversely. Indeed, it is satisfactory to have a serious soul or sound contest with one another, yet never would it be a good idea for you to disparage your companion, and absence of correspondence in marriage can deteriorate what is happening. The most effective method to Resolve this as a matter of some important thing to comprehend is that regardless of whether you are doing isolated occupations, you both are a solitary substance or fortified with affection - this implies your relationship is preeminent than whatever else. Be empowering in the event that your companion fizzles and be pleased when your mate succeeds. There is no space for any sort of examination or rivalry between two individuals who love one another. two or three mix-ups

Various Ways of Effective Communication to Strengthen Your Marriage

You can have different kinds of correspondence with your mate and reinforce the obligation of your marriage. Assuming you wish to know how to impart in a relationship successfully or how to open correspondence in a marriage, indeed, here are a few different ways you can do that:

1. Casual Communication

You examine all that is important or other senseless things that occurred during the day. You chuckle together and live it up discussing a few cheerful parts of life. This sort of correspondence assists in building a more grounded bond with your mate since you share fun and blissful minutes together.By

2. Discuss Challenges

Each marriage has lows and highs, and it is vital to examine and assess the qualities and shortcomings of your marriage with one another. Such discussions assist the relationship with developing and furthermore help with settling on any significant changes or choices throughout everyday life.

3. Nurturing Communication

This is a proactive sort of discussion that isn't incited because of some need or interest, dissimilar to the interchanges referenced previously. These sorts of interchanges stress having savvy examinations that incorporate discussing your feelings of dread, wants, dreams, trusts, and so on. This incorporates significant discussions that can prompt significant connections. These are extremely close discussions as it gives you looks at your mate's inward life.

ways of fortifying marriage

Rules and regulations to Improve Your Communication in Marriage

We will presently examine some marriage correspondence tips or a few customs that you want to practice to work on your correspondence in marriage:

1. Attempt and Be Specific

Whenever you wish to come to a meaningful conclusion, ensure you are explicit about it. Try not to skirt the real issue or discuss irregular things that are irrelevant. Abstain from summing up by offering expressions like "You generally say/do this". This may not address the reason; all things being equal, you might wind up harming your mate.

2. Be Respectful

Regardless of what sort of discussion you and your life partner are having, it is essential to be conscious towards it. By being a decent audience, you show that you regard your accomplice. At the point when you tune in, your accomplice will do the equivalent when you need to say something.

3. Try not to Nag or Taunt

Nobody likes getting singled out or annoyed, and similar turns out as expected for your mate. You can't continue to make your accomplice blameworthy or liable for his previous mishaps at whatever point you wish to come to a meaningful conclusion. Your accomplice needs to feel adored and needed, and each time you insult your accomplice, it causes hurt and agony, yet it additionally influences your relationship. Additionally, never haul in relatives or companions when you have contentions.

try not to bother or insult

4.Do Not Jump to Conclusions
Try not to expect things or concoct your own accounts without having a word with your mate. You might lash out that your mate didn't get your call without understanding or allowing them an opportunity to make sense of why it worked out. Converse with your companion about the thing that is irritating you in regards to them and knowing the reality behind their side of the story.

5. Have Regular Conversations
Regardless of how occupied you are or the amount of work you possess to do, ensure you

take out an opportunity in a day to have some significant discussion with your mate. On the off chance that you can't imagine anything to talk about, get ridiculous or senseless and share a few loud giggles with one another. It is vital to speak with your mate consistently to keep the affection streaming in the relationship.

6. No Blame Games

Regardless of whether you are frantic on the grounds that your companion accomplished something wrong, beginning looking for someone else to take the blame isn't suggested. Conceivably your life partner might have had self-acknowledgement that a misstep was committed and vital measures might have been taken to set things straight. In any case, regardless of whether there is no acknowledgement, it is in every case better to put across a point quietly and courteously as opposed to stirring things up around town individually with every one of the faults.

no attempts at finger pointing

## 7. Try not to Rely on Online Chatting

At the point when you are away working or away from home, talking through a mechanism of internet visiting is helpful to a degree, however it can't substitute significant balanced discussions or telephone discussions. In some cases online methods of correspondence can prompt mistaken assumptions and disarrays and may strain cheerful connections.

## 8. Try not to Be Defensive

In the event that your accomplice needs to draw out certain objections or issues against you, it is critical to pay attention to them eagerly without being cautious about it. It is similarly difficult for your accomplice to get their own imperfections in front of you. Ensure you tune in and go to successful lengths to settle the issue as opposed to becoming guarded about the entire issue.

## 9. Be Tolerant

We as a whole have various inclinations, likes or aversions, and the equivalent goes for two individuals who are hitched to one another. You might like watching cricket yet your mate loves tennis; be grateful and lenient toward one another's leisure activities, decisions and other such viewpoints as opposed to whining about them. Since when you become responsive, your accomplice will as well.

be open minded

10. Express Positive Feelings
The majority of us might discuss our concerns, pressures, fears and other such gloomy sentiments more than we discuss good sentiments like love, sympathy, lowliness and so forth. Ensure you incorporate more good discussions, which would incorporate commending one another, showing affection and care and other such good sentiments.

Correspondence in a marriage assumes a considerably more fundamental part than we can understand. It means quite a bit to open channels to have clear and significant correspondence with your mate so there is trust and understanding, and that implies a superior relationship with your companionJ

**Chapter two: How to Be a Better Wife and Improve Your Marriage?**

.

Marriage accompanies difficult work and the two players need to resolve to turn out to be better and become together.

**•Assume liability**

"We don't see things as they are, we see things as we are."- Anais Nin

At the point when you decide to see your significant other as your most prominent profound educator, you start to see that each upset in your relationship turns into a chance for self-improvement and for you to develop nearer all together.

At the point when I was first hitched, my better half and I would get into a ton of contentions about keeping up with and cleaning our home. I was an expert coordinator and his concept of being coordinated was the point at which his heaps of spotless and grimy garments weren't covering the room floor. This made me insane and I felt completely wrecked by his wrecks.

From the get go, it was not difficult to fault him for how I was feeling. However, that didn't feel perfect and it certainly didn't fix the messiness issue. It is generally difficult to do, however when you assume a sense of ownership with your own sentiments in a relationship, there is normally a gigantic measure of development and recuperation accessible.

At the point when I thought about what was happening in my own life that was being reflected back to me through this test, I understood that there were activities and things that were sitting in allegorical heaps, dismissed and incomplete, similar as the heaps of garments and papers that were flung about our home.

I then, at that point, understood that the heaps weren't a sentence to experience my days in a muddled home, yet rather a chance to dial back and notice the job that interruption was playing in my own life.

When I perceived this, I became inquisitive about it. Then, I addressed it by focusing on conquering my own interruption and mental mess. Lastly, I did my own "tidying up" by having a genuine discussion with my significant other where I claimed my part in the resentment and conveyed defenselessly, truly and straightforwardly about how I was feeling and what sort of help I really wanted from him.

From that point onward, two things happened rather rapidly. In the first place, the minor player quit feeling so desperate to me. Furthermore, with practically no provocation from me, my significant other began putting forth a greater attempt all the more reliably and our home began to look and feel much improved.

At the point when you will assume total ownership for your own sentiments and upset in your relationship, you won't just be a superior spouse, yet closeness and trust will begin to bloom and your marriage will prosper.

Make a dream board or an optimal scene (regardless of your Husband)
At the point when you get in the vehicle to head off to some place and you don't know precisely how to arrive, the principal thing you would do is enter the location of the objective into the GPS on your telephone or in your vehicle's route framework. In the event that you don't have a clue about the location, that will make it sort of precarious to arrive.

It's the same way with your marriage. To be in a better place in your relationship with your significant other, begin by picking the objective.

A dream board or an ideal scene can be a great method for laying out the image of where you need to go in your marriage. You will need to pick symbolism that addresses encounters you need to have or ones that summon the sentiments you need to have together.

You can likewise add words that address the characteristics you believe your marriage should have or the qualities you need to live by as a couple. Put your vision board somewhere you will see it every single day. The motivation behind why vision sheets work is on the grounds that you are basically captivating in representation over the course of the day when you check it out.

Considerations become things. Also, after a short time, you'll contemplate whether you are Alice and you've simply "ventured through the vision load up," in light of the fact that you're presently living in your own special individual married wonderland.

P.S. Your better half doesn't need to do this with you for it to work. However, on the off chance that he's down, snatch a jug of wine, your #1

Spotify playlist, and set yourself up for a wonderful night out!

**•Variety code your schedule**

Peter Drucker, the organiser behind current administration said,

"Let me know what you are worth and I could trust you, yet show me your schedule and your bank articulation and I'll show you what you truly esteem."

I frequently urge my clients to get out their schedules during training meetings in light of the fact that the manner in which we oversee and relate with our time massively affects all aspects of our life.

Spouses included. At the point when you reliably put away an opportunity for your soul mate, your marriage will normally move along.

Last year, I began coding my schedule so that initially, I can perceive how well I am dealing with my time and assuming I am living as per my qualities. Arrangements in green address time are enjoyed with friends and family and I focus on it to have a sound measure of energetic Kelly green on my schedule every week including one entire day every week shut out as a "no arrangement zone" when my significant other and I are both off.

This day is my obligation to us hanging out and having some good times together. The arrangement and variety (which reverberates with the heart chakra) are viewable signs on my schedule every week that help me to remember what is essential to me and advise me that zeroing in on my marriage is a day to day responsibility, in addition to a something to be praised on commemorations.

What's more, feel free to relinquish any tension around this at this point. It doesn't need to be resolved completely every week. Flawlessness isn't the objective. Progress is.

**•Engage in sexual relations consistently for a month**

On the off chance that you haven't yet known about "Attractive September," feel free to Google it now. I'll stand by. Well actually, I'll save you the humiliating hunt history, and the anticipation.

Provocative September is precisely exact thing the name suggests: a common and consensual responsibility among you and your accomplice to engage in sexual relations for 30 days straight during the long stretch of September. A kind of long distance race of actual closeness, maybe.

Having intercourse for 30 days in a row could sound simple to one individual, and difficult to another, even to two individuals inside a similar marriage. It takes responsibility, inventiveness, and correspondence to satisfy this test. What's more, on occasion, it can feel like sort of an errand (regardless of whether you think your significant other is smokin' hot).

So for what reason make it happen? Indeed, I figure how you do one thing is the way you do everything.

So on the off chance that you will be rehearsing responsibility, imagination, and correspondence with your significant other in the room, that experience will work out in your life outside the room too.

This will prove to be useful when you want to plunk down to discuss last month's Mastercard bills or how you will deal with special times of year this year.

Things being what they are, do you need to hold on until next September rolls around to begin with your moving around? Not by any stretch. I say don't let Pope Gregory and his schedule hinder a great time on the off chance that you like to begin now.

The main thing is to be available to learn new things about your significant other, about yourself, and about your marriage.

According to emily Fletcher, organiser behind Ziva Meditation and the Ziva Technique,

"We don't think to improve at intervention, we contemplate to significantly improve at life."

Also, I think a similar thought applies here. You don't do Sexy September to improve at engaging in sexual relations together, you do Sexy September to significantly improve at doing coexistence!

**•Gain proficiency with another dialect.**

At the point when I got hitched, my bridesmaids gave me a bushel brimming with treats that they thought would be valuable for my new life as a spouse. Wrapped up with a beautiful robe, monogrammed wine glasses and a cookbook was "The Five Love Languages" by Gary Chapman. I read it at a time and I requested that my better half perused it too.

In the book, Chapman makes sense of how every last one of us gives and gets close to home love in a relationship in an unexpected way.

The five "dialects" are "Encouraging statements," "Quality Time," "Getting Gifts," "Demonstrations of Service," and "Actual Touch."

In the wake of perusing the book, we recognized our essential main avenues for affection through a basic test and made "cheat sheets" that assisted us with distinguishing the most effective methods for communicating adoration to one another.

For instance, assuming your essential main avenue for affection is "help out," you could feel most cherished when your better half takes the trash and reuses it and adds that to your rundown. However, assuming your essential way to express affection is "Quality Time," odds are high that you'd most likely prefer he leave the trash where it is and come go along with you on the lounge chair for some discussion and snuggles.

Your accomplice might feel new to the language you get love in the event that it isn't his essential main avenue for affection or on the other hand on the off chance that he didn't experience childhood in a family where love was communicated in like that. Provided that this is true, I suggest showing restraint toward your man, as it can in a real sense feel like he is learning an unknown dialect.

I likewise began monitoring how cherished my better half was feeling on a size of 1-10. Chapman proposed asking your accomplice "how full their adoration tank is." I like to pose this inquiry a couple of times each month and when my significant other answers with a number lower than 8, I ask him how I might bring that up to a 10.

Also, assuming his number is on the higher end of the scale, I J him for some good reason so I can keep figuring out how to fluidly communicate in his language more.

# Chapter Three: Parenting

Being a parent can be dismaying. Not exclusively is your kid's wellbeing in your grasp, yet you are additionally liable for raising them well. Bringing up youngsters who are composed, dependable, yet aren't troubled by their general surroundings appears to be particularly hard. In the present age, when we are more mindful of formative brain research, being worried of having the 'right' nurturing style is totally reasonable.

## How to Enhance Your Parenting Skills

There are three regions you can focus on while attempting to acquire positive nurturing.

Presenting your kid to productive conversations is significant. The following are a couple of manners by which you can improve positive collaborations with your little one.

**1. Invest quality energy with your kid**

In the event that you have more than one kid, ensure you invest quality energy with every kid independently as well as together. One-on-one time with your kid will assist you with understanding your kid better and improve your bond also. Utilise this opportunity to energise your kid in whichever action you pick together. Try not to utilise this opportunity to address or show the kid anything, simply focus on investing energy with one another.

**2. Put forth clear lines**

Kids need structure to thrive. Clarify the standards for your kid with the goal that he/she can comprehend the reason why you have these guidelines set up and the outcomes of not having them by any stretch of the imagination. Answer any inquiry he/she might have persistently and as obviously as possible.

## 3. Get clarification on pressing issues and pay attention to the responses

Posing inquiries when your kid is youthful opens lines of correspondence that will be useful as he/she becomes older. Pose inquiries about his/her day to day daily practice and pay attention to his/her responses to start the discussion further.

## 4. Act Rightly

Youngsters are extraordinary imitators and will get propensities that they find in their environmental factors. They likewise search for what is great in individuals around them. Thus, in the event that you take the 'get in line or on the grounds that I said as much' course, your kid will be confused. He/she will likewise distrust you when you do something contrary to what you ask him/her to do and will get your propensities at any rate.

## 5. Relax responses

Youngsters and teenagers press buttons to get a response from grown-ups. While it might appear to be hard, you should keep control of your bothering and disturbance and answer them solidly yet delicately.

## 6. Try not to do everything

Your kid needs to grasp that he/she should figure out how to get abilities and care for himself/herself as well. This might be helpful for his/her future. When your youngster masters another expertise, pass on it to his/her to do it when he/she really wants to. It very well may be difficult to give your youngster space, however that is definitively what he/she really wants for a full turn of events.

## 7. Quit pestering

At the point when you concentrate on any conduct either negative or positive, that conduct will in general increment. So rather than bringing up a propensity that is unwanted, don't focus on it. All things being equal, acclaim your kid when he/she accomplishes something positive.

## 8. Handle parental struggle behind entryways

At the point when your kid sees you and your life partner contending or differing over a nurturing procedure or choice, the kid will consider it to be an opening to set one in opposition to the next to his/her benefit. All things considered, discuss your methodology with one another away from your youngster and make changes that will be to your kid's advantage.

## 9. Construct areas of strength for a framework

Try not to underrate the benefit of getting different grown-ups your youngster collaborates with. Converse with the educator, mentor, grandparents and, surprisingly, your neighbours. Keeping them in the know will assist you with understanding how your kid is creating in circles that are outside your domain. It will likewise give you an existence to get things done for yourself.

## 10. Delegate

Knowing when to assign is a portion of the fight. Acknowledge offers on looking after children find support with the tasks around the house. Nobody individual is furnished to manage the sheer measure of work that is engaged with bringing up a youngster. Get the grandparents engaged with angles that will give pleasure to them also.

## 11. Remember yourself

In some cases, in all the whirlwind of bringing up a kid, we fail to remember that we existed before the little one showed up. Take time every day with a couple of customs to support your healthy identity. Most guardians are exhausted while bringing up their youngsters. Invest energy to recharge yourself as this won't just eliminate any pressure however will likewise make you a superior parent.

## 12. Unrestricted love

Quite possibly the main thing your kid will learn is that you love him/her genuinely. In any case, it may very well be accepted that this is perceived by your youngster intrinsically. Your youngster should be shown that your affection did not depend on boundaries. At the point when you face your kid about any issue, don't track down flaws, scrutinise, or fault your kid which could cause him/her to feel under-certain. Realising there is somebody in their corner regardless of anything else, will engage your youngster.

## 13. Be friendly to your companion before your youngster

Your kid will admire you and your life partner to understand what a marriage resembles. Showing warmth that is veritable towards one another will show your kid that this is the manner by which grown-up connections seem to be.

## 14. Be steady

There isn't anything more harming to a kid than an unsound climate. In the event that your principles and conduct change consistently, your kid will get befuddled and their misconduct might proceed. You should sort out your rundown of non-debatable standards or conditions that depend on astuteness and not power. Carve out opportunities to clear up these guidelines for your youngster. The possibilities of complying with a bunch of decisions that are predictable are essentially higher than ones that continue to change to suit your requirements.

## 15. Gain appreciation, don't request it

Most guardians expect that as guardians they genuinely deserve regard from their youngster. Be that as it may, your kid won't think something similar and will scrutinise your position in the event that you request regard. Treat your kid with a similar regard and you'll track down him/her responding something very similar.

Bringing forth a sound kid and from there on ensuring that they stay solid is just a portion of the fight won. Converse with different guardians and have a sound conversation on what functions as a general practice and what doesn't. You should likewise keep in mind to not be too severe with yourself. Being a parent is difficult and you will undoubtedly commit errors. Own depend upon them and have a solid discussion with your youngster.

## Effective Parenting Skills Every Parent Should Have

Would you like to have great nurturing abilities?

Obviously you do.

You need to assist your kids with capitalising on their true capacity, and you maintain that they should be contributing citizenry.

However, filtering through all the nurturing tips out there is tedious.

Makes it seriously confounding that the tips from various "nurturing specialists" are many times disconnected!

I needed to realise what nurturing abilities and tips have been demonstrated to be viable. So I read through every one of the logical articles I could find.

In light of numerous long periods of examination, I've concocted this rundown of 12 great nurturing abilities.

.Research-upheld great nurturing abilities
To turn out to be more compelling as a parent, practice the abilities that have been demonstrated to obtain the best outcomes.

These will turn into the nurturing qualities you can then depend on to bring up kids who form into sure, fruitful grown-ups.

**Nurturing ability #1:**

Focus erring on your kids' positive way of behaving than negative way of behaving.
Yale University brain science teacher Alan Kazdin makes sense that guardians ought to be deliberate about zeroing in favouring their youngsters' positive way of behaving than on their negative behaviour.

The more guardians chasten or condemn, the more the terrible way of behaving gets rehashed.

At the point when they get a great deal of chiding, youngsters begin to incorporate the conviction that "I'm a terrible kid who makes trouble and gets chastened".

In that capacity, they don't feel persuaded to address their way of behaving, in light of the fact that it has previously turned into a piece of their personality.

Successful guardians comprehend that the better methodology is to recognize or portray their youngsters' acceptable conduct when they see it.

**Nurturing expertise #2**:

Teach your kids to zero in on the necessities of others.

Lara Aknin's examination shows that youngsters track down bliss through providing for others.

As a matter of fact, kids find more prominent joy when they provide for others conciliatorily.

These are intriguing discoveries, in light of the fact that the vast majority of us are normally egotistical. We pay special attention to our own necessities before the requirements of others.

Yet, that's what the exploration demonstrates assuming we defeat our narrow minded nature and spotlight on the necessities of others, we'll be more joyful.

Assuming that you believe your kids should lead happy, satisfying lives, help them to serve others and contribute. Include them in exercises where they get to help other people and have a constructive outcome.

At the point when your youngsters think more as far as commitment and less as far as accomplishment, they'll be on the way to building a blissful and effective life.

**Nurturing ability #3:**

Don't yell at your kids.
Mother and little girl
You've likely currently let yourself know that you shouldn't yell at your kids.

Yet, when your kids are making you bonkers, preventing yourself from yelling is difficult.

Ming-Te Wang's exploration discoveries are clear: The more you yell at your kids, the more their conduct will worsen.

Rather than attempting to control your kids' way of behaving, grasp their viewpoint and sentiments. Then, at that point, utilise consistent thinking to break through to them.

**Nurturing expertise #4:**

Give your youngsters obligations around the house.
The Harvard Study of Adult Development is one of the longest longitudinal investigations at any point finished.

One finding of the review is that kids who do more errands around the house become more joyful later on.

Family obligations show kids significant life illustrations connected with obligation, collaboration, local area and difficult work.

Individuals who learn such examples right off the bat in life are bound to turn out to be balanced grown-ups.

Fruitful guardians make family errands a piece of the family's everyday practice and culture. This sets kids up for future achievement.

**Nurturing expertise #5:**

Build areas of strength for a with your mate.
What does your marriage have to do with your nurturing abilities?

Youngsters from low-struggle families are more joyful and more effective over the long haul, when contrasted with kids from high-struggle families.

The examination shows that guardians who have a solid marriage are bound to bring up kids who are composed.

**Nurturing ability #6: Teach your youngsters to emphatically see difficulties.**

View difficulties decidedly
Eminent analyst Carol Dweck has gone through many years attempting to comprehend what your attitude means for how effective you become.

She has found that individuals who view difficulties and obstructions emphatically are definitely bound to become fruitful than the people who don't.

Fruitful individuals check out difficulties and think: "It will be hard, yet fun is going. I will gain some significant knowledge through the most common way of defeating these difficulties."

Then again, individuals who aren't so fruitful gander at difficulties and think: "It will be hard, so I'd prefer to accomplish something simpler. I'll attempt to keep away from these difficulties, yet in the event that I truly can't, I'll track down an easy route, all things considered."

These varying mentalities foster in youth and pre-adulthood. In that capacity, great guardians level up their ability of empowering their kids to decidedly see difficulties.

**Nurturing ability #7:**

Don't get things done for your kids that your youngsters ought to do themselves.
Guardians maintain that their youngsters should be capable and autonomous.

However, simultaneously, they want to regulate their youngsters intently and get things done for their kids that their kids should do themselves.

This makes sense of the predominance of overprotective guardians.

Larry Nelson's exploration shows that overprotective nurturing makes kids become less participating in school, and causes their prosperity to endure too.

**Nurturing expertise #8: Help your youngsters foster interactive abilities.**

Specialists followed in excess of 750 youngsters over a time of 13 to 19 years. They found a connection between the youngsters' interactive abilities as kindergarteners and how fearless and effective they were as adults.

These discoveries feature the significance of showing kids interactive abilities.

**Nurturing ability #9:**

 Guide your youngsters without controlling or constantly fussing over them.
Guide your kids
Analyst Diana Baumrind has done long periods of exploration about the impacts of various nurturing styles on children.

She reasoned that there are three kinds of nurturing styles overall:

**Lenient**: The parent is excessively permissive and surrenders to the youngster's nonsensical requests over and over again. The parent doesn't define steady limits or rules. Kids with lenient guardians frequently become "ruined".

**Dictator:** The parent is excessively severe, and is often unforgiving and inflexible. The parent frequently constrains or powers the kid into getting things done. Youngsters with dictator guardians frequently become angry and defiant over the long haul.

**Legitimate:** The parent is "perfect", showing warmth and fondness toward the youngster without being liberal. The parent defines limits for the youngster, however will think twice about arranging on the off chance that the circumstance calls for it. All else being equivalent, youngsters with definitive guardians are probably going to have cheerful, fruitful existences.

Besides, Wendy Grolnick's examination additionally shows that youngsters who are raised by controlling guardians are less autonomous and are more averse to foster issue solving

**Nurturing expertise #10: Give your youngsters a conviction that all is good.**

Research by Lee Raby shows that kids who have serious areas of strength for safety right off the bat in life proceed to perform better in school. These kids likewise proceed to have better connections in adulthood.

This might appear to be an undeniable finding, however it's fascinating to note that early encounters significantly affect a kid's turn of events.

**Ways to Improve Your Parenting Skills**.

**•Be Flexible**

It is never simple to Raise kids. As a matter of fact, it's not unexpected one of the most difficult — and disappointing — things you will at any point do, particularly on the grounds that you are mastering nurturing abilities as you go. Nobody goes into nurturing knowing precisely how to deal with all that is tossed at them. Be that as it may, the best guardians are continuously searching for ways of getting to the next level.

To get familiar with nurturing, you've proactively created the most vital move toward becoming the best parent you can be. Obviously, you care about how you interface with and bring up your children; that is probably the main piece of being a decent parent.

Guardians who battle with their nurturing liabilities or feel excessively wrecked to attempt to improve might be adversely affecting their children. Neuroscience research shows that when children are presented to negative encounters during their young life, it very well may be hurtful to their creating brains.

Yet, being a decent parent can balance those negative encounters — and upgrading your positive nurturing abilities is an incredible spot to begin. To assist you with dealing with reliably further developing your nurturing abilities, view this nurturing expertise agenda of six things you can do right now to be a superior parent to your children.

**•.Pay attention to Your Kids**

Have you at any point been occupied to such an extent that you don't understand your children are conversing with you? Sit back and relax — it could happen to potentially anyone. Notwithstanding, when you are investing energy with your kid, put forth a valiant effort to stay away from interruptions, including those meddlesome contemplations about work, the clothing, or your telephone that is by all accounts calling out to you.

Focus on it to understand what your children are expecting, what they dread, and what they have a restless outlook on. Tune in and clarify some pressing issues, regardless of whether they disregard you or attempt to sidestep replying. At the point when you exhibit that you give it a second thought, you are showing them that you love and worth them and their contemplations and suppositions.

Undivided attention additionally implies you centre around the thing being said without pondering how you will answer. It's tied in with watching non-verbal communication and getting on signals.

One more method for further developing your listening abilities is to get on your kid's level so you can look at them without flinching. That might mean stooping down so you match their level. Offer your children your total consideration and visually engage.

In any event, connecting and delicately contacting their arm or holding their hand when they're vexed implies that they stand out enough to be noticed, yet that you relate to what they're feeling.

**•Adhere to Your Rules**

As a parent, you must show your children the distinction between good and bad, and that implies you really want to keep the guidelines, as well. In this way, when you accomplish something wrong, commit an error, or fly off the handle, fess up. Model how to apologise, get a sense of ownership with your activities and set things straight.

You likewise should be certain your discipline is reliable yet adaptable. For example, there will be times when you'll express no to your children and would not joke about this. There will be different times when you understand you've committed an error or maybe answered too cruelly.

Assuming you truly do change your guidelines, be certain you say, "I was off-base," and make sense of why you adjusted your perspective. Likewise, recollect that we as a whole commit errors. In this way, make it a point to concede that.

Nonetheless, when the discipline fits the wrongdoing, stand firm. Kids notice irregularities and will involve them in support of themselves. Keep in mind, rules should be implemented after they are made. What's more, anything that rules are set in your home, you really want to follow them too, except if you have a truly valid justification why you're prohibited.

What Makes A Good Parent?

A decent parent is somebody who endeavours to settle on choices to the greatest advantage of the youngster.

What makes an extraordinary parent isn't just characterised by the parent's activity, yet in addition their expectation.

A decent parent doesn't need to be great. Nobody is great. No kid is wonderful either … remembering this is significant when we set our assumptions.

Effective nurturing isn't tied in with accomplishing flawlessness. Yet, it doesn't imply that we shouldn't pursue that objective. Set elevated requirements for ourselves first and afterward our youngsters second. We act as significant good examples for them.

# Chapter 4: How to make your weekends better with your kids.

"I figure we ought to discuss the end of the week," the centre points out a half year after our child's introduction to the world.

"The end of the week ... sucks," he says. He steps back because of a paranoid fear of my response.

"Gracious, say thanks to God," I say. "I thought it was simply me."

I value the centres assuming the job of Subject Broacher, which can frequently prompt one being the Couch Sleeper On'er. Truth be told, I'm regularly feeling better. My significant other expressed out loud whatever I'd been thinking. I simply didn't have the guts to just own it.

As another parent, every other person appears to be so blissful constantly. I take my children to the recreation area toward the end of the week, and the spot is loaded up with guardians who appear to be restless to go through their entire day there. Me? Ten minutes in I'm checking my watch thinking about how long until I can do something I need to do, similar to everything except watching my child play. At lunch, while my child makes a weapon of the salt and pepper shakers, different guardians close by should be visible investigating their children's eyes, saying, "I simply love the time together." By Sunday evening, I'm counting the minutes until Monday morning, when I can return to work and unwind.

My better half asks why I held on until he raised the subject, "On the off chance that you were hopeless, for what reason didn't you tell me?" he inquires.

"I didn't realise I could," I admit. "I never realised I was permitted to despise something about being a mother. I believed that implied I was a terrible mother."

So we dive into an exceptionally extended, and extremely legitimate, conversation about how to make our family ends of the week better. The centre needs more opportunity and feels remorseful for not needing his life to consist of work and time with the children as it were. I need to work out, invest a little energy alone, or even better, with the paper. We both need to invest energy with our child, together and separated. We simply don't have any desire to invest all our end of the week energy with our child, together or separated.

Since we've been investing so much energy doing what we would rather not do, we choose to speak the truth about what we would like to do. We choose to attempt to plan our life to be loaded up with what we maintain that it should be, not with what we don't maintain that it should be.

This is the way we figured out how to make due, and appreciate, ends of the week with our children.

## 1. Ease up!

Set free on the standards, and infuse somewhat more fun into your ends of the week. Offer yourself a reprieve from being required to uphold the principles, and offer your children a reprieve from being required to live by them. This might mean you have a "Rug Picnic" breakfast before the TV (your child, not you), "Senseless Sunday" (breakfast for supper) or "PJ Mornings" (which might endure well past lunch). You can definitely relax, come Monday early daytime all that will have returned to ordinary, and your children will not necessarily anticipate cupcakes for breakfast.

## 2. Try not to exhaust.

An exhausted mother is an exhausted youngster, so fill your ends of the week with stuff you really prefer to do with your children. Try not to "stomach it out" only for sitting back. There's no honour function on Sunday night for the most hopeless mother, so do what you like to do.

## 3. Make arrangements.

Most guardians see ends of the week as, "How long until Monday?" Instead of hanging tight for it to end, make arrangements with different families and companions with whom you and your children appreciate investing energy. Also, at any rate, there's security in larger groups. A greater number of guardians are superior to one, and it eases the pressure off of you.

## 4. Pay off the youngster.

Without a doubt, we would rather not use treats, TV, or later sleep times as remunerations for good ways of behaving. But toward the end of the week when we've worked the entire week, we haven't had one moment to plunk down and we truly need our child to take that treat, TV or later sleep time in return for an issue free end of the week. So on the off chance that the youngster watches some additional TV while you do the New York Times crossword puzzle, have at it. Simply don't anticipate that your baby should help. Those riddles are extreme!

## 5. Request downtime.

It's nurturing, not jail. Most working guardians will admit to feeling staggeringly remorseful for not having any desire to constantly enjoy their end of the week with their children or mate. Tell the truth and let your life partner tell the truth, as well. Assuming you love that twist class, plan it in and leave father home with the youngsters. Assuming he cherishes that tennis match-up and hates to miss it, give him your approval. By giving yourself and your companion the consent to invest energy doing different things than nurturing, you'll partake in the times you are nurturing significantly more.

## 6. Find support!

We consider her the marriage saver, the school young lady who comes over a few Saturday mornings and spends time with our children several hours while my better half and I both would do things we like to do — separate from our children, and J for a very long time and I would rather not stop. My better half loves his morning tennis match-up and makes the opportunity to help him to de-stress from a hard week at work. I don't loathe him and nor does he hate me since we're not leaving the other hanging. The remainder of the end of the week is "everyone ready and available," and we love it.

Ends of the week as a parent of small kids are not what they used to be. Gone is the space to marathon watch your most recent garbage TV fixation, partake in a tedious side interest, or recuperate from a headache in harmony.

All things considered, your ends of the week become principally about engaging those little youngsters. Also, it doesn't make any difference how tired you are from the week from heck, your children will be chomping at the bit to go. You should unwind at the end of the week, yet I ensure your children will have another thought.

## 7 . Don't Give Up!

Easygoing weekend life isn't finished. You're not surrendered to 10 years of 7-days seven days depletion (despite the fact that that is the means by which it could feel at this moment). You simply have to rebalance a couple of things, and become better about how you deal with your family at the end of the week.

The most effective method to unwind at the end of the week when you have children

.

In the first place, Think About Your Weekend Mindset

Ends of the week have changed since having children, that is guaranteed. Thus, have a go at moving the manner in which you view ends of the week now as well. It assists with tolerating that the programmed personal time you used to have won't occur on its own any more - BUT it can in any case work out assuming you make it.

Assuming you just consider the end of the week a trudge of playdates (for more youthful children), being a taxi administration (for more seasoned children), and swimming through errands, then, at that point, that is the way your end of the week will work out. That is the means by which it will FEEL - like a trudge with nothing else in it to appreciate. However, recall you merit time to unwind and re-energize, so begin focusing on your unwinding time as a non-debatable piece of your end of the week.

On the off chance that you're routinely counting during the time until Monday morning when you can get away from back to attempt to unwind, then, at that point, now is the ideal time to make a move. Rolling out unobtrusive improvements and preparing to make ends of the week more adjusted and charming takes practice, however should absolutely be possible. (Alright, perhaps few out of every odd end of the week, since life occurs - yet it very well may be done a ton of the time.)

Keep in mind - there won't be a prize giving service on Sunday night for who had the most hopeless end of the week, so don't feel remorseful about rolling out certain improvements so you can partake in your time off more.

Unwinding at the end of the week as a parent
Relinquish High Expectations
In the event that you continually feel like the end of the week is squandered/upsetting/unsuitable, inquire as to whether you're coming down on. Is it true that you are expecting a lot of yourself and of your downtime? Assuming you're

reaching skyward as far as the amount you can finish or the amount you need to unwind, you'll generally wind up frustrated.

Attempt re-evaluating your assumptions for the end of the week, and what's practical with a youthful family close by. In the event that you have little kids, it's illogical to accept that you can figure out how to paint the house, have a party, get the week's things done, and go on a climb at the end of the week. Pick several of those things, all things considered, and really do them.

Be kinder to yourself. You don't have to accomplish all that at the end of the week.

To finish, plunk down and plan out how you can sensibly get past them over the course of the following couple of ends of the week, while still figuring in a chance to unwind to the recreation prepare brownies go cycling/sleep/go out for frozen yoghourt. Focus on the things that you really want to do, and a few things you need to do.

## Ease Up - For Your Own Sake As Much As The Kids

The weekend is your personal time. And keeping in mind that we as a whole realise that children will more often than not flourish with schedule, make sure to allow things to go unnoticed a piece over the course of the end of the week. Let a relaxing of the principles become the end of the week schedule. Why? Since loosening up the principles implies more diversion for the children and less pressure for you.

You don't have to allow bedlam to dominate. In any case, consenting to a PJ day, a rug outing breakfast, a film supper, a wear-whatever-you-like day, or whatever else you can imagine gives an important encounter to the children while really easing the heat off you.

Kids playing while guardians loosen up toward the end of the week
Split Your Weekend Time
No one needs to plan and coordinate the entire end of the week, however having an unpleasant arrangement can truly assist with giving you an opportunity to focus on the things you need to do. On the off chance that you don't make arrangements for it, it's doubtful it will work out.

It additionally truly helps on the off chance that you can split your time into which parts of the end of the week will be family time, time for yourself as well as your accomplice, and an alone opportunity to truly turn off. Preparing isn't precisely unique and unconstrained, yet it's likely your most obvious opportunity with regards to really getting what you look for from the end of the week.

Try not to Schedule Kids' Activities all weekend long
Kids will generally have a ton of exercises at the end of the week. Sports, playdates, birthday celebrations and so on are terrifically significant pieces of your children's lives however they all stack up, and in the event that you're not cautious they can undoubtedly wind up assuming control over the entire end of the week, leaving you broken down (and perhaps a piece angry).

So give your best for keep responsibilities booked to one day please. Clearly this isn't generally feasible, however making anything that strides you can to restrict them to one day will give you a free timetable to fit in time for everybody to unwind and re-energize. Or on the other hand attempt to fit them in on mornings just, leaving the evenings free for some family time or alone time.

Recall it's likewise thoroughly fine to express no to additional responsibilities. In the event that your end of the week is as of now looking full, don't feel regretful about turning down any additional ones. The more things you join to, the less opportunity you must unwind.

Give Everyone a Say in The Weekend's Activities

Not all ends of the week are occupied. At the point when you have a peaceful end of the week without much arranged, take a stab at asking everybody what they might want to do that end of the week, and integrating some of everybody's thoughts into the preparation. Indeed, even young children will actually want to express an inclination of some sort or another.

The fundamental thing to recall here is that YOU count as well! The magnificence of this straightforward activity is that it offers the grown-ups the chance to examine what they ask for from the end of the week, and the children get a feeling of decision while finding out about compromise.

Track down Ways To Balance Everyone's Fun

Since you're set on accomplishing something the kid is well disposed of doesn't mean it can't be a good time for you as well. Engineer your end of the week to make the youngster exercises include something agreeable for you too. Pick the delicate play with the best bistro. Pick the recreation area with the best espresso truck. Pick exercises where you can drop off the children and work on something for yourself. My significant other has found a dance class for my girl which happens at a close by college grounds with running paths, so he goes for a run while she moves.

Making exercises perform multiple tasks likewise saves time, and is critical to a superior end of the week for everybody.

Getting Time For Yourself At The Weekend

Take turns with your accomplice to get alone time. Also, don't feel regretful. You shouldn't feel terrible for not having any desire to spend each and every waking snapshot of your end of the week with your loved ones. This doesn't make you a terrible parent. As a matter of fact, whenever you've had a break, you'll be a far superior parent. Take the time. Re-energize.

Consent To Trade Lie-ins With Your Partner
Kids not actually into dozing late at the end of the week? Thought not. Alternate getting up with them on Saturdays and Sundays, so it is possible that you or your accomplice can return to rest.

Effectively tire The Kids Out

With any karma you're anticipating a smidgen more margin time on Friday and Saturday nights that you ordinarily get during the week. Increment your possibilities of a smooth sleep time by figuring in some sort of daytime movement that will leave the children tired. Ideally something on the outside, and on the off chance that you get to plunk down during it, all the better.

## Make Friday or Saturday Nights a Little Bit Special

One of the real factors of nurturing life is that Friday and Saturday evenings will generally be to a great extent equivalent to the wide range of various evenings. You could remain up somewhat later, you could have a glass of wine, however in the end you're likely sitting on the couch staring at the TV once more.

Have a go at effectively making Friday or Saturday nights a piece not quite the same as each and every evening of the week, regardless of whether you're staying put. This is particularly significant during the pandemic while going out for a night out on the town feels like ancient history. Alternate cooking a new thing, requesting a focal point from some place you've been needing to attempt, set up a video call with companions, do a virtual action together, or attempt one of these at-home night out thoughts.

Getting time for yourself at the end of the week

Take advantage of Family Weekend Time
Before I had youngsters, I cleverly felt that guardians went through the end of the week avoiding the recreation area with their child who-never-have-fits, prior to getting back to their perfect, clean homes to get a continuous night's rest. Definitely.

You can envision my shock when the truth hit me and I was confronted with the sheer fatigue of being a functioning guardian in a real sense simply attempting to limp as the weekends progressed.

Sounds natural? Some of the time it seems like there's no time at the end of the week to appreciate everyday life since you're utilising the entire chance to get up to speed from the week. Try not to surrender: attempt a couple of basic strategies to finish stuff early so a greater amount of your end of the week can be utilised for no particular reason family time.

Use Friday to Get Organised If You Can

Take a touch of time on Friday nights (even 10 minutes will assist with doing) all the figuring out school bags, lunchboxes and so on and get as much ready for the following week as possible. This will mean you're on the ball on Sunday - particularly valuable assuming you're inclined to the Sunday night blues.

Likewise, assuming you're telecommuting on Friday, have a go at booking a staple conveyance that day so you don't have to go through hours in the general store at the end of the week.

Fit In Chores and Errands Where You Can During the Week

You could have the option to fit in two or three things to a great extent during the week, yet each and every piece will help. A room vacuumed on Tuesday night is one less space to vacuum at the end of the week. Attempt to go to the mail centre or drop off the laundry on your mid-day break. What's more, get however much you can convey or use click and gather, since shopping trips with little kids are typically distant from unwinding. Continuously follow the easiest course of action.

Then, at that point, at the end of the week attempt to corral tasks and tasks into one time allotment just, similar to Saturday morning or Sunday evening, to abstain from letting them assume control over a great deal of the end of the week.

Prepare If You're Going Out For The Day

It takes something beyond snatching your telephone and keys to escape the house nowadays. Getting out for the day with small kids requires stuff, and more stuff, and latrine trips, and returning for a most loved toy, and failing to remember things.

Help yourself out and prepare on the off chance that you're going out for an end of the week road trip with the children. Gather a sack the prior night.

Attempt to eat a dinner out of the house

An existence with little youngsters includes a great deal of food prep, table clearing, surface cleaning, and creeping around on the floor getting the perpetual stream of food that individuals have tossed there. A simple method for easing the burden at the end of the week is to eat one feast (or more!) out of the house. Not pondering what you will cook, or lift it up off the floor a while later, is off the charts valuable. One of the significant things I missed during the pandemic is having lunch out in a bistro on Saturdays or Sundays - it truly makes a difference.

# Chapter five: 10 Ways to Strengthen a Marriage and Avoid Divorce

It requires work to secure, support, and grow a marriage. Between work timetables, youngsters, and different commitments, once in a while it can appear to be difficult to keep up with that organisation. At the point when issues emerge, a few couples see that as it's better to separate and go their different ways.

For other people, dealing with the relationship is a superior decision. If you have any desire to remain with your accomplice and keep away from each other, there are proactive measures you can take. From further developing correspondence to injecting more sentiment into everyday life, the following are 10 methods for working on your association.

**1.Focus on your relationship**

Playing with the possibility that you may be in an ideal situation beyond your marriage can overburden your relationship — regardless of whether you never voice those contemplations. As a matter of fact, the idea alone could make a significant break in your inspiration attempt to work on your marriage.

To battle the gamble to your relationship, choose early that separation isn't a choice. Committing to the responsibility will assist you with zeroing in on making your association more grounded as opposed to pondering what life may resemble outside your marriage.

**2.Honor and Respect Your Partner**

Individuals unavoidably change over the long haul. Understanding, appreciating, and adjusting to those changes is basic for any relationship. Begin by making a rundown of your accomplice's most desirable characteristics and help yourself to remember the magnificent individual you wedded. This exercise will assist you with recalling why you fell head over heels for them in any case.

It additionally assists with expressing the amount you value your accomplice's peculiarities and eccentricities.3

Tell your accomplice consistently — through praises or expressions of gratitude — that you value all that they do.

These little articulations resemble stores in the bank. You would rather not make withdrawals from your marriage while never putting aside any instalments. Thus, be certain you are doing things that honour your accomplice for who the person is.

## 3.Impart Regularly

In the age of cell phones, Netflix, and telecommuting ways of life, it's not difficult to get diverted. You could find that you frequently go days without having a genuine discussion with your life partner.

Conveying straightforwardly about your life, interests, dreams, disappointments, and sentiments is a significant method for encouraging closeness in a relationship.

It's likewise significant that you additionally stand by listening to your accomplice voice their contemplations. It may very well be useful to save 30 minutes every day — liberated from Interferences or interruptions — where you can talk.

## 4.Share Financial Expectations

Numerous relationships are laden with conflicts over finances. Couples frequently achieve various assumptions to cash in on a relationship. Each accomplice can find it challenging to see what is going on from the other individual's point of view.

Coming to an understanding about how your cash will be dealt with is a basic part of a fruitful marriage. Settle on a spending plan, a way to deal with obligation, and make an arrangement to live inside your cutoff points.

It's likewise critical to separate among needs and needs. While both are authentic, couples can deal with issues in the event that they attempt to satisfy every one of their needs disregarding their financial plan.

Consolidate an adaptability in your financial plan to consider diversion, gifts, excursions, and different exercises that will reinforce your marriage.

**5.Give Each Other Space**

One of the hardest things to adjust in a marriage is the perfect proportion of time to spend together. An excessive amount of can want to cover while too little can be deciphered as negligent.

At the point when your accomplice needs space or a night out with companions, propose to watch the children or get the things done to guarantee they can get that time. Then again, you additionally need to make time to enjoy with your accomplice. Assuming that keeping an eye on or monetary requirements make that troublesome, plan a tomfoolery, savvy night out at home.

The key is that you both put forth a deliberate attempt to hang out while likewise permitting each other the space to have an outside community.

**6.Work on Wellness**

It's not difficult to get into a daily practice of being excessively easygoing, particularly on the off chance that you've been with your accomplice for a long time. A simple method for reviving sentiment is to recall those beginning of dating — planning for night out with an at-home nail trim, getting a new shave and hair style, or picking a tomfoolery outfit.

There are a lot of ways of feeling appealing and stimulated. Staying aware of your actual wellness supports your certainty and feeling of well-being. It can likewise serve as a method for investing energy with your accomplice — whether you're attempting another exercise class, preparing for a 5K, or preparing good dinners together.

**7.Have Date Nights**

One more method for keeping the fire consuming in a marriage is to keep pursuing your spouse.8 Try to set aside a few minutes for a night out each week — regardless of whether it's simply to get frozen yoghurt or cook another recipe together. In the event that cash is a worry, consider exchanging minding another couple hoping to have a night out. You can likewise place the child in a buggy and go for a stroll around the shopping centre or go to the recreation area.

Keep doing the things you did when you were dating. Many couples report that little acts of kindness assist them with feeling like love birds. Take a stab at leaving your accomplice little love notes where they will track down them, make them espresso in the first part of the day, or purchase their  nibble at the supermarket.

## 8.Excuse Quickly

Relationships frequently start to go to pieces when one individual is holding resentment. Research has shown that feeling disdain toward your accomplice quite often putrefies and can prompt separation assuming it's never resolved.

Attempt to excuse your accomplice as fast as could really be expected. Recollect that pardoning is the same amount of a gift you give yourself. Holding resentment occupies mental and profound room and quite often influences your wellbeing and stress levels.

Settle on a generous soul and you will receive the positive rewards, be it better rest or stress help.

Assuming you have violated your accomplice, genuinely apologise and request their pardoning. Truly pay attention to what they need to say and attempt to comprehend the reason why they are disturbed. Tell them you will chip away at how to do things another way later on.

Try not to Try to Control Your Partner
In solid relationships, the two accomplices have common regard for each other and don't request their own specific manner. This can mean various things to various couples, however here are some centre occupants to remember:

**9.Try not to attempt to screen or control one another.**

Give your accomplice space to be the individual they are.

Figure out how to team up on major choices (like burning through cash and bringing up kids). Allow your life partner to have the opportunity to travel every which way without asking your authorization.

Accomplices who endeavour to control each other gamble turning out to be genuinely oppressive. They could show indications of monetary maltreatment — which every now and again prompts separate.

## 18. Track down Help

Assuming you're actually having difficulties in your marriage or you dread that separation may be unavoidable, consider mentoring or couples therapy. If you don't know where to look, begin by checking with your work environment. Check whether you (or your accomplice) approach a representative help program (EAP), which can frequently guide you to starting assistance or give a reference.

On the off chance that you and your accomplice share confidence, think about gathering with a confided in a strict pioneer.

Does Marriage Counselling Work?

Exploring issues in a marriage can be challenging. To endure in the relationship and forestall separation, the two accomplices need to focus on accomplishing the work and investing energy and exertion. While the objective is to save the relationship, you will eventually need to choose if remaining together is the ideal decision for both of you.

In the event that you and your accomplice need more assistance, think about working with a marriage mentor or a strict pioneer on the off chance that you share a similar confidence. These people can assist you with getting another viewpoint and can direct you to extra administrations if necessary.

## 6 Steps for Resolving Conflict in Marriage

Scarcely any couples like to just own it, however struggle is normal to all relationships. We have had our portion of contention and a portion of our conflicts have not been pretty. We could presumably compose a book on what not to do!

Begin with two childish individuals with various foundations and characters. Presently add a few unfortunate behaviour patterns and fascinating characteristics, toss in a lot of assumptions, and afterward turn up the intensity a little with the everyday preliminaries of life. Prepare to be blown away. You will undoubtedly struggle. It's inescapable.

Since each marriage has its strains, it's anything but an issue of keeping away from them yet of how you manage them. Struggle can prompt an interaction that creates unity or confinement. You and your mate should pick how you will act when struggle happens.

**Stage One:** Resolving struggle requires knowing, tolerating, and acclimating to your disparities.

One explanation we have struggle in marriage is that opposites are drawn toward each other. Normally an errand situated individual weds somebody who is more individually arranged. Individuals who travel through life dangerously fast appear to wind up with companions who are more slow paced. It's abnormal, however that is essential for the motivation behind why you wedded who you did. Your companion mixed it up, zest, and distinction to your life that it didn't have previously.

In any case, in the wake of being hitched for some time (some of the time a brief time), the attractions become anti-agents. You might quarrel about little disturbances —, for example, how to appropriately crush a container of toothpaste — or over major philosophical contrasts in dealing with funds or bringing up kids. You might observe that your experiences and your characters are different to the point that you can't help thinking about how and why God put you together in any case.

It's critical to grasp these distinctions, and afterward to acknowledge and change in accordance with them. Similarly as Adam acknowledged God's endowment of Eve, you are called to acknowledge His gift to you. God gave you a life partner who finishes you in manners you haven't even advanced yet..

We were no special case. Maybe the greatest change we confronted right off the bat in our marriage outgrew our contrasting foundations. I experienced childhood in Ozark, Missouri, a little town in the southwestern corner of the "Show-Me" state. Barbara experienced childhood in a nation club setting close to Chicago and later in Baytown, Texas. Barbara came into our marriage a refined young woman. I was a certifiable hillbilly.

It was like we came from two unique nations with very surprising customs, legacies, propensities, and values. The distinctions became obvious from the get-go in our marriage. Take furniture, for instance. Barbara had an Ethan Allen dream book and she was continuously checking it out. It was brimming with things made of strong cherry, strong pecan, strong mahogany. It was nothing for seats to cost $189.95 — per leg.

I didn't have the foggiest idea why she needed to go purchase this sort of stuff when, in southwest Missouri, you could go to K-Mart and get a formica table with chrome legs and six seats! What's more, for significantly under $189.95. You can eat off that sort of table for quite a long time and it won't ever show any wear.
All in all, how could we think twice about? We purchased a collectible and I was supposed to restore it — which set out a freedom for one more significant distinction in our experiences to surface. Barbara's dad was an architect. He is precisely gifted, can fix anything, and really

appreciates it. I'm persuaded he could fix an atomic reactor.

My father had experience with deals. Fixing things was not his concept of tomfoolery. In the event that bailing wire or a little channel tape wouldn't work, he typically called the handyman or anything that repairman was vital.
Thus we were right there, recently wedded, with an old fashioned table that required resurfacing. I went at it hesitantly, yet I made it happen. Somehow or another it saved our marriage in the early going.

**Stage Two:** Resolving struggle requires overcoming narrow-mindedness.
Our disparities are all amplified in marriage since they feed what is without a doubt the greatest wellspring of our contention — our childish, wicked nature.

Keeping up with amiability in marriage has been troublesome since Adam and Eve. Two individuals starting their marriage together and attempting to go their own childish, separate ways can never expect to encounter the unity of marriage as God planned. The prophet Isaiah depicted the issue precisely over a long time back when he portrayed fundamental human self-centeredness like this: "We all like sheep have gotten sidetracked, every one of us has gone to his own particular manner" (Isaiah 53:6). We are egotistical; we as a whole intuitively pay special attention to number one, and this leads straightforwardly to struggle.

Marriage offers a gigantic chance to take care of self-centeredness. We have seen the Bible's arrangement work in our lives, we're actually seeing it work day to day. We have not changed one another; God has changed the two of us. The solution for finishing self-centeredness is tracked down in Jesus and His lessons. He showed us that as opposed to needing to be first, we should be last. Rather than needing to be served, we should serve. Rather than attempting to save our lives, we should lose them. We should adore our neighbours (our companions) however much we love ourselves. So, if we need to overcome narrow-mindedness, we should surrender, yield, and give it all.

As Philippians 2:1-8 tells us:

Subsequently assuming there is any support in Christ, in the event that there is any reassurance of adoration, assuming there is any cooperation of the Spirit, assuming any warmth and sympathy, make my delight total by being in total harmony, keeping up with a similar love, joined in soul, aim for one reason. Don't do anything from childishness or void pride, however with modesty of psyche see each other as more significant than yourselves; don't simply pay special attention to your very own advantages, yet additionally for the interests of others. Have this disposition in yourselves which was likewise in Christ Jesus, who, despite the fact that He existed as God, didn't respect uniformity with God a thing to be gotten a handle on, however purged Himself, appearing as a bond-worker, and being made in the similarity of men. Being found in appearance as a man, He lowered Himself by becoming faithful to the place of death, even passing on a cross.

To encounter unity, you should surrender your will for the desire of another. Yet, to do this, you should initially surrender your will to Christ, and afterward you will track down it conceivable to surrender your will for that of your mate.

Snatch some guidelines to change your battles into correspondence leap forwards.

**Stage Three:** Resolving struggle requires seeking after the other individual.
Romans 12:18 says, "In the event that it is conceivable, however much it relies upon you, live serenely with all men." The more I experience the more I understand how troublesome those words are for some couples. Living serenely implies seeking after harmony. It implies stepping up and determining a troublesome clash as opposed to trusting that the other individual will venture out.

To seek after the goal of a contention implies saving your own hurt, outrage, and harshness. It implies not losing heart. My test to you is to "keep your connections current." At the end of the day, resolve that you will stay in strong partnership everyday with your companion — as well similarly as with your kids, guardians, collaborators, and companions. Try not to permit Satan to acquire a triumph by segregating you from somebody you care about.

**Stage Four:** Resolving struggle requires adoring a showdown.

Wordsworth said, "He who has an old buddy needs no mirror." Blessed is the marriage where the two mates feel the other is an old buddy who will tune in, comprehend, and deal with through any issue or struggle. To do this well takes adoring a conflict.